The Light and Depth of Mirrors
Creative Reflections on Women and Self-Esteem

Edited by
Anne M. Talvacchio
Project Director
Pennsylvania Division AAUW
Creative Woman Project 1987-89

AMERICAN ASSOCIATION OF UNIVERSITY WOMEN
2401 Virginia Ave., N.W.
Washington, D.C.
20037

Library of Congress Catalog Card Number: 89-60512

ISBN 0-9611476-1-X

Printed in the United States of America

Table of Contents

Preface

Unlike windows, prisms, telescopes, magnifying glasses, spectacles and other seeing devices, mirrors focus our vision inward rather than outward. Subjecting every image to a variable blend of truth and distortion, mirrors expose us to ourselves. Those made of glass reflect the "objective" physical self. Other mirrors are composed of personal experiences in which thoughts, motivations, and quirks of personality are revealed. Many times our likenesses are projected back to us by other people — family, friends, strangers — who respond to the many different faces we wear in public.

Yet virtually no glimpse of ourselves, however chance or cursory, goes without judgment. How do we measure up: against our own ideals and dreams, against the expectations of others, against the standards of our time and culture?

This book is a collection of personal viewpoints about the way women develop a sense of self-esteem out of the multitude of self-images they see reflected around them. It is, therefore, a book filled with feeling: pride, hope, doubt, fear, guilt, and determination. Not only does the poetry, fiction, nonfiction, and illustration speak directly of the risks and rewards of the search for self-esteem, but the process of creating this body of work was one which dared Pennsylvania AAUW members to scrutinize their own self-images and share their insights in creative ways that would challenge thought and emotion.

The 1987-89 Creative Woman Project of the Pennsylvania Division of the American Association of University Women (AAUW) was designed to serve two purposes: One, to provide a forum of creative expression for its members, and two, to produce original materials which could inspire and direct reflection on the subject of women's self-esteem.

Entries were juried anonymously for artistic quality and relevance to theme. In addition to myself as project director, jury members included: Annegreth Nil, assistant curator of contemporary art at The Carnegie Museum of Art, Pittsburgh; Alice Brand, published poet and director of writing at Clarion University; and Gwen Lawrence, former facilitator at the community college level for women setting new career and education goals. I thank them for the time, expertise, and enthusiasm they gave to the task.

My grateful acknowledgement also goes to the Pennsylvania Division Board of Directors for its support and encouragement throughout all phases of this project.

i

I believe that all who participated in this endeavor will have gained that special sense of satisfaction that comes from braving both private introspection and public review for the sake of their growth as creative women. I hope that their creativity encourages us all to continue exploring and developing our own unique insights, talents, and skills — which is what being an AAUW member is all about.

ANNE TALVACCHIO, *Project Director*

The Light and Depth of Mirrors

Creative Reflections on Women and Self-Esteem

Pathways to Self-Esteem

MARTHA RAAK, *Greensburg Branch*

For the last three summers, a colleague and I have had the privilege of spending one intense week with a dozen or so high school age women discussing and experiencing choices and the process by which one makes wise personal and educational decisions. In preparation for the program, each girl interviews women about their views. Inevitably, the interviewees stress to the girls the power of education, of meaningful work, of marrying later rather than earlier in life, and often state "be true to yourself." Apparently, many of these women feel that they were trapped in an early marriage and are personally unfulfilled.

Listening to these words and reflecting on the many adult women with whom I've worked, I feel that confidence and goal-setting are key factors in building self-esteem.

I believe that, traditionally, most women have sought fulfillment through others—be it their husband or children. Much of their energy was focused on these "other" beings. Many bright women have put their husbands through medical or law school only to be discarded at a future date with a now-professional husband saying, "she hasn't grown with me." Children may or may not fulfill one's lofty expectations given the distractions and seductiveness of today's glitzy world. I do not propose abandoning one's responsibilities or being unconcerned with satisfying family relationships, but I do suggest defining oneself—"who am I"—and setting some goals as crucial steps on the journey toward self-esteem.

Knowledge of one's own values is another important pathway on the journey. What is important to you? Money, recognition, helping others, power, leisure time, learning, social life, friendship, spiritual life, family time, prestige, making the world a better place? The more you define your values, the greater the congruence between your inner feelings and the outward manifestations of them in your life.

For example, let us say that you have always wanted to be a writer. Do not let any excuse stay your hand. Set a goal and put it in writing; "I will write at least one page, five out of the seven days each week." Then do it! Remember, you do not have control over others, but you do have control of yourself. What a marvelous feeling it is to put something on paper and then do it. Achieving goals is a powerful way to develop self-esteem.

A third pathway is to become freer, more playful, more risk-taking. Often, a person will become freer with age. There is a realization that pleasing oneself is a key to a successful life and that life has a natural rhythm. To live life to its fullest and to experience other cultures, people, and places is a joy. Hang glide, travel, try a new recipe, learn a foreign tongue, go somewhere by yourself — in short, risk making a mistake or a fool of yourself. A no-growth attitude is one where change is resisted. Yet the ability to adapt to constant change is a mark of an assured and flexible individual. Accepting others is another indication that one accepts, loves or esteems oneself.

Life is a search for meaning; meaning is derived through actualization. Therefore to possess self-esteem is to be en route to self-actualization. Self-actualization occurs as an individual balances personal needs, values and goals and is content with her present state of existence, yet striving for a loftier one.

35

Not burdened down by graying hair
or small repairs that need be made
or all the signs of growing old
presenting their birthright.
Never with such fervor have I looked upon my life.

A threshold to cross, a path stretches out
to meet the sky.
A woman becomes a dove, a swan, an eagle.
There's more to learn than stars.
A new-found impetus starts the quiet
stringing of the heart.

All the parts become a whole.
Wife, mother, student, volunteer,
friend, establishing a new career.
A soul that's learned to love this life,
Find beauty in a face.

Faith and truth take on the task
of going forth in quest
of peaceful heart and active mind
before the winter's rest.

I like this time, with all its faults and
decisions to be made.
And savor the quiet confidence with
which I view my life
at thirty-five.

KAY PETTY MOORE, *Eastern Delaware County Branch*

The Last Slumber Party

MARY LYNN H. ELLIS, *NEMCO Branch*

When are a bowl of popcorn, pajamas, and oldies on the radio the props for a conjurer's trick? When they magically transport a group of women to a place in their own distant pasts: a slumber party.

What had begun as reminiscing over wine-coolers on a summer afternoon had somehow become real. Here we were, aged thirty-three to forty-seven, running up the path to a friend's house on a rainy Friday night with toothbrushes, sleeping bags, and casseroles for breakfast under our arms.

On the table was a big bowl of popcorn. Just like in the good old days. But there was also guacamole and hot crab dip. The oldies on the radio were older than ever, but we hadn't forgotten the dances that went with them: line dances, the twist, the stomp.

Topics of conversation were familiar too. We talked about guys, school, our bodies, love. Of course, these days the guys were our husbands, ex-husbands, and sons. The teachers were our kids' teachers. We joked about our looks, some in mock despair, some seriously hurt by the betrayal of our once lithe bodies.

At one point the talk turned to abortion. But where we had once argued with intellectual and moral intensity on one side or the other, now the debate was quieter, more emotional. Each of us knew someone who had been faced with that immense decision at some point in her life. It wasn't hypothetical anymore.

Romantic dreams of the future, which had preoccupied so much of our conversation back then, were absent from this evening's discussion. We knew so many things now that we hadn't then. We had all hoped for love. We hadn't known that love would warm some of us like a hand-stitched quilt and sear others like a blowtorch. Back then we were our mothers' children. We had not yet conceived of the metamorphosis that would change us into our childrens' mothers. We hadn't known what far cities would claim us, what men, what books we would or would never write.

One thing that hadn't changed at all, however, was the laughter. At midnight, four of us in slinky nightgowns, dangling rhinestone earrings, and long white gloves did our rendition of the Supremes' "Stop In The Name Of Love." It was as sophomoric and uninhibited as fun gets. One person in the audience "laughed 'til her head hurt."

Only half of us actually spent the night. The half who left had their reasons: preference for a familiar pillow and mattress, husbands with early morning plans, husbands who couldn't handle the idea of a wife sleeping anywhere but beside him.

That was another thing. Surely none of us ever called home from a pajama party when we were sixteen. Who cared what Mom and Dad were doing? For wherever we were was the center of the world. But there were several calls to check on things at home and one early morning dash across the street to feed the kids before sitting down to breakfast with us. The center had definitely shifted.

We who stayed spread our sleeping bags on the rug at 3 A.M. When two friends got an attack of giggles in the dark, the laughter rippled all along the line of bodies in a flash of déjà vu. For a little while, we *had* gone home again.

But that's when the biggest difference between then and now surfaced. It was utterly impossible for a bunch of grown women to sleep on a hard floor. We tried, but one by one we crept off to empty sofas and beds. By morning, we looked and felt like we hadn't slept at all.

As we rolled up our sleeping bags and moved the furniture back into position, it was agreed that the best parts had been the food and the laughs. The worst, a unanimous vote, was sleeping on the floor. Never again, we vowed.

Still, we were glad we had done it — made the trip back through our memories, through our common history as girls-becoming-women. Because we discovered something we had then that we still have now: a sense of sorority, the pleasure of sitting around a living room in our pajamas, sharing secrets, eating popcorn. Women together. While the rest of the world sleeps.

But it was the last time. We need our sleep. And more than ever, we need our dreams.

Thoughts on Passing a House on Valley Street

Perfect

Was the structure.

Scrubbed

Rinsed

Painted

Papered

Right down to mulched

Telephone poles,

But it was not

Home.

CAROLE BRIGGS, *Brookville Area Branch*

The Russians and Me

BERNICE KING, *NEMCO Branch*

Mikhail Gorbachev and I are partners in glasnost, both of us busily restoring truth to history after years of revisionism.

I come from a family who habitually lies about their age, both men and women. Age is treated as something akin to a fault, a dirty secret. During a recent visit my 85-year-old father whispered to me, "Don't tell Ben (his 58-year-old friend) I'm in my 80s. He thinks I'm in my 60s." It's true my father doesn't look his age, but I'm sure Ben knows he is old. I watch them together and see that Ben treats my father with deference, great care and much patience. Ben kindly slows his movements to match my father's so that my father has the illusion they are age peers. However, Ben's affection for my father comes from their shared enthusiasms and great compatibility, and has nothing to do with age.

Later in reviewing family news, my father tells me of a recent photo of Aunt Louise (80 years old) and how she "looks really old!" When I remind him she is old, he counters, "Well, Lily (his sister) is 92, and *she* doesn't look it." Somehow it's as if Aunt Louise is a failure because she looks all of her 80 years.

Aunt Louise, a matter-of-fact women who faced life with simplicity and good heart, never made a pretense of her age. Marriage to Uncle Mel was not easy. She spent 40 years carrying out commands that always started with "Loo-eee-saa. . . . " Uncle Mel loved good times and, as the life of any party, was a free-spender. But it was never Aunt Louise's party. It was her job to somehow keep the house going on whatever he deigned to give her after his good times rolled. Aunt Louise deserves a summa cum laude in management. One year, in addition to making all her own and daughter Doris's clothes, she somehow miraculously made a new living room sofa. Now that's management! Later in life Aunt Louise took on a second career; she moved to California to raise six grandchildren while her daughter worked as a high school teacher.

Naturally all those years of caring and work are going to leave a little wear and tear on the face and body. Why shouldn't she look her age!

The memory of Aunt Louise brings to mind wonderful Christmas dinners at her house with Uncle Mel, Cousin Doris, and Marie. Marie, a distant relative who always came alone, dressed glamorously all in black, matching her glistening hair and framing her ivory skin. Marie was a little plump, full of laughter and lusciousness. She would regale us with detailed stories of going to the theater in New York and cooking little midnight suppers of squab and wine with her lawyer friend, Claude. Marie and Claude were magical to me in those Depression times when my father was only working two days a week, when I had never been to the theater, let alone tasted squab.

Marie never told her age. No one was even certain of it when she died. To this day she is greatly admired, and this mystery of her age always mentioned by the family.

My sister, Jane, who takes after my father — looking years younger than her age — keeps up the family litany that if you confuse the facts enough the truth will never out. She claims her California friends think her 20 years younger, and that not even her 41-year-old son knows her true age.

Jane taught me this family gospel well, and for many years my faith was untouched. I kept quiet about my age, never mentioning it to my son. But the older I got the more questions arose, the more complicated it became. How was I to reconcile dates in yearbooks, diplomas, marriage license, years teaching school, 11 years as a free-lance editor, and many more in advertising? What was I to leave out? The numbers never jibed. Like a pre-Gorbachev historian, I had to decide what had to be expunged from the records, what monuments defaced.

The deception became ridiculous, self-demeaning. So, despite the power of family myth, I finally came out of the closet, dragging sister Jane behind me. Now I find myself in the unique position of being older than my older sister, and also something of a spoiler, a strange crank. This becomes most vivid at party times when I correct men who are explaining something that took place during my era and who say flirtatiously, "But you wouldn't know about that, since it's long before your time."

Surely my family is a little addled on this subject, but they do mirror the world around them. Our society is geared to the young, so much so that there is a sense of shame in admitting one is aging. My father thinks the world is a young man's game and, naturally, still wants to be counted a player. But he is a player, no matter what his age. And so is my sister, and so was Marie.

The last time I saw Marie, she must have been in her early 70s. Her dress and hair were still all black, her skin very pale, her mouth painted bright red. Claude, who I had long since realized was her married lover, was dead. But despite her caricature looks, the laugh remained. Gradually Marie, the magic player in that delicious game of entice and allure, soon wove us into her tales of life and love.

Our deceptions about age do not fool the young, and certainly not each other. So why do we continue?

Mikhail and I believe the truth shall set us free — free to take hold of the future. I disavow none of my years, erase no glyphs. It is up to me and to you to show each other and the young that in addition to blips in memory, sagging flesh, tired faces and all the other stigmata, age can also include continued curiosity, intense spirit, accumulated wisdom, and self-respect.

The Spider

Today I saw a spider cling;
Her web so new and glistening;
A work of art diminutive,
A creature's soul so primitive.
Her only purpose was to plan
A mural perfect in its span,
A show across the grass.

Reluctantly I hurried on;
There was no time to dwell upon
That fragile, splendid spidering.
My hands began to work again
To gather clothes before the rain,
But somewhere deep inside my brain
A web began to spin.

SUSAN WERTZ, *DuBois Area Branch*

SPIDER by Marianne Fyda, *DuBois Area Branch*

Conversation with My Mother

CYNTHIA GORDON, *Easton Branch*

$\mathcal{M}$other. Mother. Mother.
Yes?
Mother! You answered!
I have been answering you. You haven't heard me.
Why can I hear you now?
Because you are starting to listen. I haven't been very far from you. Don't you remember when I told you I would never be very far?
Yes. Sometimes I remember, but it is usually when I'm deeply troubled. Missing you seems to make problems worse.

Mother, why did you go? It seemed so wrong, like something that was not supposed to happen, a mistake. Like the lines of a play that had become garbled. Even now I have trouble saying it: "My mother died." Those are words that should never be used together, because they convey no meaning. My mother and death are not compatible.

I didn't want to leave you. You and your father and your brother were all that I wanted. I tried to disobey; I tried to stay with you, but in the end I was reconciled. Only — I could not quite accept how your father would face it, at least not for a long time.

Mother, I tried to deny it. I tried not to grieve. I wanted to do everything you would have been doing if you had stayed here. I tried to *be* you, so that I would not have to mourn for you.

There were times that I felt angry — angry with you for leaving me. You left just at the time I was trying to change from being a daughter to being a wife. When you left I felt an overwhelming sense of guilt, as though in trying to put my trust in my new husband I had abandoned you, and was being punished by losing you. See, I still can't say "punished by your death." Those are ridiculous words.

*What you are saying **is** ridiculous. You have no need to feel guilty. Don't you remember when your grandmother died, and I told you that regret is always a part of losing someone you love? Even when you have given fully of your love to that person?*

Yes. I remember that. But you always insulated me from anything that was really tragic. You always helped me plan how I could help heal a situation, even when I was the cause of the hurt. How could I plan for myself when you were gone?

But you did. You did plan, and you did carry out many of the things I would have done.

Mother, do you know about the things I have been doing? Can you know what is happening here? Where are you?

I told you — I am not far away. I am changed, but still the same. You can't understand, because as yet you can't see what it is that really composes a person. You see only what your eyes see, not the idea that is the person, the person that is the idea. But you will. You are closer than you were.

Mother, can you see me? My life? Every day?

Not as you imagine. I cannot "see" you as I would see a movie; but I am in contact with you. I can still help you. Not through supernatural occurrences, but through love.

Mother, you said you are changed. I want you just as you were.

Of course I am changed, dear, or else I would really be dead. That is the only way to keep from changing, to be dead. I'm surprised you asked me that. I kept changing while I was with you, didn't I?

Yes. I guess it is extreme selfishness, but I never did want to give up anything I ever had. And I certainly didn't — don't — want to give up any part of my mother. I can still feel the outrage I felt after you went. Someone, something had robbed me of what above all was my birthright: my mother.

*You mean, your birthright is your mother's **love,** and that is true. It belongs to you and nothing can take it away.*

Oh Mother, sometimes I can almost understand that; but there are other times when I am just angry. You should have stayed here. You should have been with my father to keep making him happy, to see me grow into a good marriage and to enjoy my little children with me. My life would have been so much easier, so much happier if I could have had you for a few years more.

Are you feeling sorry for yourself? Or for me?

Both, Mother. Why did it happen? Could I have done anything to keep you here? Was it my fault?

That kind of question comes close to blasphemy. You need to accept the fact that you are not all powerful, that even your love is subject to a higher power. Did you do all that you could, in love? You know you did. But having me say that isn't going to help you straighten out your feelings. You will have to do that yourself. You need to realize that part of your bewilderment is because you felt I was almost all powerful, and then found out, when I had to leave you, that I wasn't.

But Mother, why? Why so much tragedy? Why did you have to leave your family just as they were grown, when you could have had happy years of fulfillment, knowing how well your efforts succeeded?

*Why. What a question! If you are going to ask "why" then ask also why I was so blessed with the many happy years with your father when you and your brother were growing up. **Why** is such a self-pitying word. There are so* *many people and situations in the world worthy of your constructive pity that you never need to waste it on yourself.*

Mother, I try. Sometimes I think I succeed. But why am I still mourning after all this time?

Did you forget: "Blessed are they that mourn. They shall be comforted." Did you think that mourning is not a necessary part of life? All of us must learn how to mourn. Can you imagine a person being fully human who has not mourned someone beloved? You always tended to expect the ideal, and to think of any deviation from your notion of perfection as an error. That was why it was so hard to satisfy your wants when you were a child. Your father used to say that there was no end to what you wanted. Of course, to be fair, I was a little like that, too.

Oh Mother, it was always for us that you kept wanting more, not for yourself.

My dear daughter, my own little girl, that is just what we have been talking about — love. That is what love is. Accept it; it is yours.

Revolution or Evolution?

JOAN JACKSON JEFFERS, *Pocono Area Branch*

–I–

God-fearing and resolute, Euphemia left a highland croft in 1890 to serve in a "great house" in Glasgow. She found her destiny in a ship's captain twenty years her senior.

Adapting methods learned in the great house, she created a comfortable, well-regulated haven for kith and kin. Together they prodded nine "bairns" into right relationship with God and man. Industry, integrity, loyalty, hospitality, and thrift were virtues to undergird a life and glorify God.

Sabbath was set aside for worship (three services, including one in Gaelic), personal renewal (reading and the weekly nap she allowed herself), and family (the simmering stew could somehow be stretched to feed one more guest). Her kettle was always "on" and her time, energy, and resources were available to family and neighbors in need.

When the Great Depression savaged Britain, they braved an ocean to afford their brood greater opportunities. She was widowed at fifty, barely settled into a new house in a new land. Euphemia opened her door to young immigrants, providing a foothold for them and modest income for herself. 28 Sunset Avenue became the hub of the growing, transplanted clan. Her faith, strength, competence, and warmth nourished them all.

Eleven of her fourteen grandchildren and one great-grandchild found comfort in her ample lap and guidance in her sage advice before her death almost thirty years later.

–II–

God-respecting and with lively intelligence, Effie learned the household arts at Euphemia's knee, helping to mother the six younger than she. Heeding paternal cautions to "be sensible," she mastered Gregg and accounting for her livelihood, lavishing her talents as a couturiere solely upon her sisters.

In America, she chose her partner with deliberation, selecting a persistent suitor with lofty ambitions. He had pursued her since childhood summers in Saltcoats and had also come to the United States to better provide for his widowed mother and sisters. He established a rising business career while Effie established a well-ordered home with well-disciplined daughters.

Over the years, her social graces enhanced his progress while her management ability maximized their growing income. With the girls in school, she resurrected her office skills to aid his fledgling proprietorship, negotiating flex-time and family Friday dinners out as benefits.

She encouraged her daughters to use their minds and talents in socially responsible ways. Stereotyping and ethnic slurs were met with reproof at a time when the social upheaval of World War II encouraged such attitudes. Church attendance was expected, as were charitable attitudes and acts, but slowly more secular recreations became the means to recharge waning energies. Music, literature, and theater were valued, presenting new opportunities — and choices.

Widowed at fifty-four at the crest of their success, Effie ran the business for a year and retired to being mother, grandmother, sister, friend. "Never bored with my own company," she read, crocheted, knitted, traveled, and nurtured grandchildren, free now to follow her own inclinations.

A giver, she found it difficult to receive. Even her death, sudden and solitary, reflected her fierce determination to rely only on herself and God.

–III–

God-loving and tenderhearted, Joan was free to dream in the ordered security of Effie's cocoon. Her shy gentleness was protected by aunts, uncles, cousins.

Books, movies, and theater were her windows on "reality"; MGM musicals and Rodgers and Hammerstein plays spun illusions of "happily ever afterward" as an antidote to the harsh realities of World War II and its aftermath.

Encouraged and admired for her academic bent, Joan ventured off to a respected university. Heeding fatherly cautions to "be practical," she majored in secondary education rather than literature. Emerging and stretching newly found wings in the stimulating atmosphere, she plunged into campus activities (Christian Association, PanHel, camp counselor to disadvantaged children), discovering a sense of power through service. Her memorial to her father, who died midway through her sophomore year, was to excel. The awarding of her bachelor's degree, a family first, was a source of pride to the whole clan.

The struggle to transmit the thrill of Shakespeare and the satisfaction of coherent expression to provincial youths ended with marriage to an upward-bound charmer and motherhood. Periodic returns to the classroom were prompted by financial dictates, and she concerned herself more with the mental health than intellectual prowess of students, having observed first-hand how vital affirmation is to developing psyches.

Choosing not to compete for the Immaculate Housekeeper Award, Joan described their home as "clean enough to be healthy, dirty enough to be happy." Their three children led less-ordered lives than hers had been but had more freedom to explore many avenues and to make mistakes. Each blossomed into a distinct individual with talents different from either parent as well as shared interests and abilities.

Her husband's mid-life crisis provided new ground for growth, not entirely welcome. The purchase of a small motel required extending the "open door" formerly offered to friends to accommodate strangers. Adjusting to life "on call" and "at your service," Joan acquired management and accounting skills, and witnessed dimensions of human nature she had only known through books. She saw herself as a proprietor who happened to be chambermaid; her husband saw himself as a custodian who happened to be proprietor. Six years later, they emerged wiser, she stronger and relatively intact.

Briefly they relished freedom to travel, read, or simply "be", until financial pressures and family circumstances forced them back into the joint yoke of job-holding and care-giving. His heart-attack and the daily presence of an aging parent brought home the fact that her own life was probably two-thirds spent. She had "shown . . . spirit and power; but had hardly . . . been on (her) own line," as Matthew Arnold said in "The Buried Life." Only after attending to the perceived needs and expectations of parents, husband, children, friends did she feel free to attend to her own neglected dreams.

Slowly Joan is learning to say, "I'm entitled," "There are alternatives," "We both can have our way." Threads from the past interweave with threads from the present to form the fabric for an integrated future.

–IV-A–

God-embracing and confident, Meredith encounters life with open arms and dancing eyes.

In childhood, she sampled a smorgasbord of opportunities with large helpings of music, service, and communication. Her energy and empathy found various outlets from assisting Joan with UNICEF and the Fresh Air Fund to theater productions to editor-in-chief of the school paper.

Determined to be her own person, she distanced herself geographically at age eighteen. Blocked from becoming a music therapist by musical perfectionists, she willed herself through college in three years, an assortment of jobs, and seminary. She would return home briefly to lick wounds or share joys but would be mistress of her life, whatever the cost.

One of Gail Sheehy's "paranurturer's," she tends her flock. Communicator, administrator, social worker. Painful self-examination and the gift of empathy require fortitude and courage. Mentors encourage her to develop more patience and greater tolerance — with herself, as well as others.

Her God is inclusive, embracing all sexes, races, abilities, and socioeconomic classes. Healing and empowering people is the focus of her fledgling ministry. Not yet thirty, Meredith confidently and consciously affirms herself and her gifts.

God-accepting and with lively senses, Melanie drinks deeply of what life offers. Her flame burns brightly.

With a drive for physical expression, she successively enjoyed ballet, gymnastics, and running, learning to control her lithe body as she matured. Her sense of color, line, and rhythm revealed themselves at an early age. Coupled with an aptitude for math and management, Mel's artistic flair leads her to plan for the day she will own her own florist shop – or chain of shops.

Enjoying the comradeship of male company, she is by turns romantic and "one of the guys," at ease in both roles. Her wardrobe ranges from the demure to the casual to the sophisticated. Tenderhearted, loyal, and intuitive, she establishes close relationships selectively and deliberately. A fiesty streak protects her from those who presume to take advantage of her tender side.

Melanie's spiritual nature is often masked by her people/action-oriented style, but surfaces in her delight in color, scent, and texture, her sensitivity to wounded beings, and her innate sense of morality.

On the threshold of assuming full responsibility for her destiny, she has her dreams, plans, and a sound sense of who she is.

* * * * * *

So we have two contemporaries, very different, yet self-aware and confident. Even in her uniqueness, each encapsulates Joan, who encapsulates Effie, who encapsulates Euphemia. What is self-esteem? Accepting one's past, affirming one's present, anticipating one's future.

My Winter Deer Trail

DECEMBER

The snowprint stitchery of a deer path
Lures me from foot familiar trails
And leads me across ravine dips and ridge rises
Amid trunk-spires and twig-traceries
Into the ice prickle snowsparks of discovery
. . . Becoming "my winter deer trail."
A sanctuary for all seasons,
Where loosened mind-threads
Intertwine with all life networks:
Enriching awareness

FEBRUARY

The last parchment leaves twitch in the wintry gusts
Emitting death-like rattles.
Tree skeletons stand stripped, night black against twilight tones.
My footsteps scatter dead leaf-scraps.
Am I alone alive? In breathing pink.
. . . Not so! The forest lives in muted rhythms, waiting.
The buried seed, the wrapped cocoon, the winterbuds, waiting.
Waiting for the earth to turn and raise its shadow side
In season's cycle:
Connecting patterns

FEBRUARY by Betty Lou Dell, *Fox Chapel Branch*

APRIL

Inspired, I lean back to see the "hanging tree,"
An ancient, shattered oak.
Splinters from its severed stump stab the sky;
Yet, from that broken trunk, a solitary branch juts out
    Then splits in two.
The dead end dangles like a hangman's noose, swaying;
The other end waves budding leaflets
Proudly, like banners on a grim battlefield.
. . . Holding life aloft on a battered base, it persists, exists:
Uplifting survival

OCTOBER

The beech's pewter roots embrace the earth for nurture and support.
Cradled among them, I too am anchored
Against earth-clay, encased in flesh-clay.
I rest, bedded in bright leaves from the glowing canopy above
Where golden flakes break free and spiral giddily
In final dancing descent.
Like autumn leaves, my thoughts detach
. . . Earth-born, not earth-bound, they soar through space
In tune with the stars, a tiny elemental pulse:
Radiating harmony

ANY MONTH, ANY YEAR

True to Nordic legend, I add a touchstone to this natural cairn,
My guidemark for departure and return.
On these elusive deer trails, everchanging:
A tree falls; a tree grows; a run-off changes course.
Young deer cut their own paths.
Time and season alter the landscape.
Nature is not constant.
Every walk is a new walk, in a new day, in a new world.
. . . In all, I am a wanderer; but
Being is enough

BETTY LOU DELL, *Fox Chapel Branch*

ANY MONTH, ANY YEAR by Betty Lou Dell, *Fox Chapel Branch*

The Metamorphosis

ELIZABETH FRANCHINI, *Harrisburg Branch*

Life has its seasons for change. Some are desirable, others not. Some are by choice, others by chance. Whatever the circumstances, the hands of time cannot be turned back. The control that we seek can come only through the perceptions of the mind, but that can be one of the most difficult tasks that life has to offer.

Little did I know five years ago that my life would begin this incredible journey that would bring about changes only once dreamed of. The local community college afforded me the opportunity of breaking the monotony that had accompanied my being "just a housewife." My youngest child had begun kindergarten, and the extra time loomed over me heavily as did the knowledge that I was ill-equipped for the changing job market.

One course in freshman psychology whetted my appetite for more, and of course, my ego was given a great boost when I was the only one in the class who was exempt from the final exam because my previous grades were so good. Could this feeble brain that had not studied in 13 years be salvageable? Maybe there was hope.

The next couple of years brought great enjoyment and great sadness to my life. As a part-time student, the challenge of mastering new knowledge and skills overshadowed the confusion over which direction to steer my education. The break-up of my marriage also brought a darkness into my life that made it increasingly more difficult to see the brightness that would inevitably follow. The details are unimportant, but it became the driving force that pushed me to levels I had never thought possible.

Taking charge of my life, putting the pieces back together again and trying to form order out of chaos became a priority over the next three years. Education became one of the few positive aspects of my life during this period as did a project for nontraditional students which included my debut as an actress. The college had hired a playwright to write a script intertwining the lives of older students. Much to my surprise, after I had revealed many of the painful details of my broken marriage, I was given the lead part in the play. Although not totally autobiographical, it gave me the opportunity to portray the difficulties many women face when they desire to become educated. It had a cathartic affect on me and made me feel as though others might be spared the difficulties I had had.

My graduation brought new hopes and new fears to the surface. My last year there was spent reaching deep into my own psyche to determine where the next phase of life would take me. Also, looking into my purse made me realize that there was not very much to take me where I wanted to go. In doing research, the Criminal Justice Program at a nearby university had great appeal to me because of my interest in working with delinquent children and the study of law and human nature.

The financial aspect was overwhelming at first, but that, too, began to fall into place. Through the thoughtful guidance and encouragement of the financial aid officer at the university, my plans began to materialize. However, there were still some personal doubts which pushed me further. Careful research of my own revealed private sources of funding. Much to my amazement, after completing the tedious and time-consuming process of applying for scholarships, several were awarded to me. The pressures began to lessen.

Doing an internship through the community college and working part time over the summer helped to ease the mounting anxiety that was beginning to build as the time came nearer to entering the university. Not only was I going to finish my degree, but I was doing it full time, commuting an hour each way, taking care of two kids, a dog, and a house. Was I crazy to think this could be done?

Maybe so, but nevertheless, the first year passed and was successfully completed. My sense of accomplishment soared when I made the dean's list both semesters, and my kids did not starve or suffer any ill effects. As a matter of fact, they are quite proud of me. My son will be embarking on his own college career in the not-too-distant future and considers me the "resident expert" in English and math. My daughter completed a year of Girl Scouting earning several badges and creating lifetime memories of the 900 boxes of Girl Scout cookies in our house when her troop needed a "Cookie Mom."

Of course, none of this could have been accomplished without a change in priorities. My kids are helping with the cooking and laundry, and are learning to be flexible. Grocery shopping is a once-a-month chore now. "I don't want the cereal that's in the house" has become a common complaint. "Tough, eat it anyway" is a typical response. The house is not as clean as it used to be, but we are all a lot smarter and happier.

Not having my family in the area makes it difficult at times, but Mom and Dad can still give me the boost I need, thanks to the phone company. Once in awhile, it is nice to feel like a kid again and have Mom tell me to go do my homework, even if it is long distance. When I do see them, it gives me such pleasure to see how proud they are of me for finally finishing college, which I never quite got around to doing when I was younger. For Dad, who was an immigrant to this country over 80 years ago, it is the fulfillment of the American dream.

Being a senior this year brings about new uncertainties. Graduation will come sooner than expected, and job hunting will be the next challenge. But the enjoyment of learning has come back now that I know the impossible has been accomplished. Growth is not as painful as it once was. The seasons for change in my life may not coincide with society's expectations, but for me they are right. I used to wish I had a crystal ball to see the future, but now I think that would spoil all the fun.

It's Just a Little Insignificant Job

My job doesn't have a lot of status
   (In the public eye, that is)
There are many others like me
   (Whose job is service)
I stand on my feet for a lot of hours
   (Sometimes busy, sometimes not)
I get very tired
   (Not just in my feet)

But it is an interesting job
   (Because of the people I meet)
I have to pay attention to their needs
   (And not just for clothing)
Once I found out that a very pleasant woman
customer had recently lost a grown daughter —
Once I helped a woman find sale items while she told
me she had just had a nervous breakdown —
One woman who has had a stroke always comes
shopping alone, asking no quarter —

And then there are the husbands
   (Most are really helpful and give good opinions)
Just a few try to make jokes at someone
   else's expense
My job may be insignificant
But I feel it is mutually rewarding
   to me and to my customers
And I feel that it is a microcosm of life.

BARBARA S. FREESTONE, *Harrisburg Branch*

Ph.D.

I sleep with my books

    nestled beside me

    thick with poetry

    rhetoric

    MLA handbook

    between glossy white covers

a cold comfort.

JACE CONDRAVY, *Grove City—Slippery Rock Branch*

A SPIRITUAL HAVEN by Laura J. Hollingshead, *Makefield Area Branch*

Sentimental Journey

VALERIE S. MALMONT, *Franklin County Branch*

Somewhere in the ugly urban sprawl which connects Philadelphia with New Jersey, the train, which had been barely moving, finally grinds to a complete stop. The interior lights go out, and it is all too obvious that the air conditioning system has also failed. Outside, a half dozen or so railroad workers are using shovels and picks to repair a section of the track.

"How long's it gonna be, Daddy?" whines a twelve-year-old Cindi Lauper look-alike. Her dyed red hair is shaved nearly to the scalp on one side, displaying a long dangling rhinestone earring. The rest of her hair defies gravity thanks to a frizzy permanent and lots of mousse. She appears to have sprung from a music video, much as Athena once sprung from the brow of Zeus.

"How the hell should I know." Her father turns to his wife. "If we'd driven to New York like I wanted, we'd already be there. I don't know why I went along with this stupid idea of yours, just because you had a great time on a train about thirty years ago." He does not expect nor get a response from the woman sitting next to him staring out the window.

He jerks open his copy of the *New York Times* so violently that the front page rips down the middle. He opens it to the financial section and tries to read it by the light of the late afternoon sun.

She sees the workmen and remembers. *Somewhere, just outside Riverside, the train had stopped. The interior lights went out that time too, as did the air conditioning. Outside, a half dozen or so workers were using shovels and picks to repair a section of the track.*

One of the men stood a small distance apart from the others. He had dropped his pick to wipe the sweat from his face with a red and white bandanna. The thumb of his left hand was hooked into the waist of his faded jeans, pulling them so low in front that it seemed impossible that he could be wearing any underwear.

His upper body was naked, deeply tanned and glistening with sweat — every muscle perfectly delineated. Golden curls framed the perfect masculine face of my daydreams.

His eyes scanned the stalled train lazily, until his attention was caught by the sight of the dark-haired, thirteen-year-old girl who was watching him through the train window. When I saw that he was looking at me, I smiled at him, and he smiled back at me.

He was the most beautiful man I had ever seen. I wondered how old he was — somewhere between his teens and manhood — perhaps twenty. Only seven years older than me. When I would turn twenty he would only be twenty-seven. Not too old for me at all.

At that moment there was nothing I wanted more in this world than to be embraced by those bronzed muscular arms. What would happen, I wondered, if I simply walked to the back of the car, opened the door and climbed down?

I imagined what would happen if I went to him. He would take my hand and lead me to a secret place, known only to the two of us, where I would live, waiting each day for him to come to me. Then one day, when I was twenty, he would put a ring on my finger and we would live forever in a house of glass overlooking the ocean.

What would happen to the people I left behind? Would my grandparents be frightened when I didn't get off the train in Chicago? Would my father cry for his lost daughter? Would my mother turn my bedroom into the sewing room she said she had always wanted? Would anyone feed my cat?

The train lurched forward a few feet and stopped again. I was only a few feet away from him and I could see that his eyes were aquamarine blue, rimmed with long dark lashes. He smiled at me again, displaying perfect white teeth, and raised his hand to wave at me as the train started to move again.

I dared to blow him a kiss. He caught it with his raised hand and brought his fingers to his lips. I watched him until he was only a speck on the horizon. I went to Chicago, and I grew up, but I never forgot his face.

"Mom, can I have some money to get a snack? I'm starving."

The woman turns from the window and regards her daughter with a blank stare. Could that pouting, painted adolescent with the exposed navel really be her child? She had prayed for a child to love for twelve years, and finally her miracle baby had arrived when she was least expected. Even then, everyone said she looked just like her father. And when she got older she acted just like him too, and the woman still wishes she had a child to love.

"Here," she tells the child, handing her a bill. "Get a sandwich. We're so far behind schedule that we probably won't have time to get dinner before the show." They have hard-to-get tickets to see *Cats* that night.

Her husband slams his paper down. "Great — that's just fucking great! Six hours of torture on this train to get from Harrisburg to New York and now I won't even get dinner!" To his daughter he says, "I'll go with you. I need a drink." He doesn't invite his wife to go along.

I was her age then. Thirty-four years ago — more than a lifetime in some countries. I wonder where he is now. What would he be doing with his life. He would be fifty-four now. The same age as my husband! But he wouldn't be bald. I was sure of that. God wouldn't have pulled that joke on him — not when his hair had been so very beautiful.

I also know with certainty that he had only been working on the railroad tracks for the summer. He would have gone back to finish college in the fall — UCLA, or perhaps even USC. He would live in a glass house overlooking the ocean, and would still have the perfect body he had when he was twenty. He has not married, of course, because he is still haunted by the memory of the dark-haired young beauty who once threw him a kiss from a train window. He thinks of me every day, just as I think of him.

His face will naturally look older now, his cheekbones more prominent, and of course there will be lines etched into his forehead because he has spent so much time in the sun. He will still be handsome, but in a more distinguished way.

I wonder if he ever does think of me — that one little face in one little window. For me he was a once-in-a-lifetime happening, but he must have seen thousands of faces looking out from thousands of train windows. Could any one face be remembered? Could he have forgotten me, when I have spent so many years remembering him?

Her husband sits down heavily, jabbing her in the ribs with his elbow. His bald head glistens unattractively with sweat, and his breath smells of bourbon. She looks at him and wonders if he had ever been young and muscular, and if his hair had ever been golden. He had been twenty-nine when she met him — already looking and acting middle-aged. He was an accountant with a large manufacturer of farm equipment. She had never dated anyone else, and after a dull courtship, they had settled into a marriage that was even duller. She now realizes that she married him because there was no one else. She had been terrified of graduating from the college which had prepared her to do absolutely nothing with her life. That was the way it had been in the fifties. She doesn't know why he married her.

He has risen slowly but steadily in his company and at fifty-four is its comptroller. His salary is high for the small town in which they live, and he trades in his car for a new one every three years.

Every day he reads the financial section of the newspaper and he has a subscription to *Sports Illustrated*. That is the extent of his reading. He makes all the decisions in his home and is very glad that his only child has inherited his practical mind rather than being a book-loving dreamer like her mother.

If I had gotten off the train, I wonder what my life would be like now. We would have loved each other with the kind of passion that only comes to the beginnings of people and never dies. Perhaps I would really have written the books I once dreamed I would write. Perhaps we would have bought an island, where the sun is always warm and the water in the lagoon is so clear you can count the shells on its sandy bottom. We would swim there naked and make love on the moonlit sand. But I hadn't left the train, and I had married an accountant and I have never swum naked or written a book or made love in the moonlight.

The train lurches forward, and the lights come on in the car.

"We should be in New York City in about twenty minutes, folks." The conductor moves down the aisle with great speed, ignoring the questions of the passengers.

Her husband pushes his bulk out of the seat and begins to pull their suitcases from the overhead rack. One side of his wife's suitcase catches him on the side of his head. It is that old-fashioned blue kind with the white trim that she had bought to carry on their honeymoon. It came with a matching overnight case, and she had felt very elegant with her matched luggage. The overnight case was last used when she took it to the hospital where her daughter was born.

"That damn thing nearly killed me. I don't know why the hell you had to bring that heavy thing along. We've got these nice canvas bags I bought at K-Mart. They don't weigh anything at all."

The train plunges into the darkness of a tunnel, and he sits down quickly.

I once read an article that told of a subterranean Manhattan, where there are levels upon levels of corridors, deserted and forgotten railroad tunnels, heating ducts, sewers and underground rivers. There are rumored to be rats as big as dogs living down there. And alligators, flushed into the sewers by young owners when they were no longer cute pets, are supposed to grow into giant monsters.

I know there are people down there too. People, who for reasons only they know, have left the world of light for life in the perpetual darkness. Their eyes adjust to the dark, like cats' eyes, and they can move through the labyrinths to any place in the city. They can even get into the buildings through long-forgotten basement entrances.

The train jolts to a stop and the car lights go out again.

"Holy shit!" Her husband pounds his arm rest with a closed fist. His wife is frightened by his violent temper. He has been known to hit her, and then make her see that it is her own fault for being so stupid.

"Daddy, aren't we ever going to get there?"

"Shut up. How do I know if we're going to get there. This whole ridiculous trip was your mother's idea. She had some kind of wonderful time on a train when she was a kid, and she wanted to experience that thrill again. Some damn thrill this is!"

I know that below the man-made maze lie ancient caverns. For thousands of years water has flowed in a dark river down to a sunless sea. The only light there comes from bits of sparkling phosphorescence — stars on the midnight-black water. Fish with no eyes live there and the underground people catch and eat them. Stalactites hang from the roofs of the caves, long calcified fingers embedded with gleaming crystals. It is always quiet and peaceful there.

"Excuse me," she says to her husband. "I need to go to the rest room."

"You won't be able to find it in the dark."

"I have a flashlight on my key chain." She switches it on to show him. He doesn't get up, so she climbs over him, taking care not to bump him with her purse and get him angry again.

She follows the tiny spot of light to the rear of the car and finds the rest room is occupied. She stands near the platform door, waiting her turn and is bumped by the conductor as he enters the car. She catches the door and holds it open, hoping some cool air will come in.

The conductor's voice comes to her from very far away. "There's no need to worry folks. Just a temporary malfunction of our electrical system. It'll be fixed in a few minutes and we'll pull into the station a minute or two after that."

The heat is becoming unbearable. She steps onto the platform connecting two cars to get some breathable air. The tunnel is blacker than a starless night, but her eyes adjust to the darkness quickly, like the eyes of a cat. She switches off her tiny flashlight.

She sees a small, very narrow ledge running along the side of the tunnel wall. Off to her right yawns a shadowy entrance to another tunnel. *Now I know what scientists mean when they talk of "black holes."* She opens the door to the outside and finds the air is cool and musty. It smells of urine, and there is another odor too.

A freshly dug grave. Why should I think of that? Something moves in the other tunnel. She hopes it is a repairman. She knows that her husband will blame her if they miss the show, and she also knows that he will punish her.

She waits, but no one comes out of the tunnel. She can just barely make out a male figure, standing still in the shadows. There is a brightness around his head, as if his face is framed with golden curls.

I could get off this train right now and walk into that tunnel and never be seen again. Nobody will ever know what happened to me. I'll find the other people who have already left the upper world, and I will move silent with them through tunnels and caverns down to the underground sea. I will take off my ugly clothing and swim naked, and I'll never put them on again. I will swim and walk and my body will become strong and firm again, and they will make me a princess. We will creep into jewelry stores through their long-forgotten subterranean entrances and I will drape my body with gold and precious stones.

The man is still standing in the tunnel entrance, watching her. Now she can see perfectly in the dark. It is a young man, wearing low-cut jeans. He is naked from the waist up. His hair is gold and he appears to be about twenty.

He has been waiting all these years for me to take another train trip!

He raises his hand to his mouth and blows a kiss to the woman on the platform. She reaches for it and presses her hand to her lips. The train groans as if it is about to move.

I lost him the last time by not being brave enough to get off the train, but he has waited for me all these years and I am not going to lose him again.

He extends his arms — waiting to embrace her, and she steps down from the train, happier in that moment than she has ever been before.

The police at first think she committed suicide by deliberately jumping in front of a train on the adjacent track. But her husband and daughter convince them that she was a content person who had no reason to kill herself. And they truly believe this because neither of them knew her.

A thirteen-year-old girl in the next car tells the police she saw a man with golden hair standing in the entrance to a tunnel. She said he had raised his arms, gesturing to the woman to close the door. The girl did not tell them that he was the most beautiful man she had ever seen, and that just a moment before the tragedy he had blown a kiss to her through the train window.

No one else on the train saw the man.

The woman's death was officially declared to be an accident.

Red Poppy

If it were Christmas Day
and on a whim you painted your fingernails
"red poppy," all that day
they would beckon like bright marble eggs
you would want to gather into your apron.

If you were to play "Are you my mother?"
your sons' new game, you would choose
the white hen on the red magnet
to match your nails. You would win,
forgetting to glide the long way home
with your lost chicks.

You cannot hold a glass of white wine
the same way when your nails are red
or lift a lighted match to candles
on the mantel. They ignite.

Dressing becomes theater. Slowly
you pull on hose like a dance girl
in a frontier saloon, hook easily
the clasp on a gold bracelet,
watch your fingers linger on the tops
of your legs as you smooth out the wrinkles
from a white silk skirt.

But if the next day you chose
to stand in front of the red plastic goal
with its white net and your sons kicked
soccer balls at you with all their tiny might
you would forget the nails, catch and kick
and never notice small red slivers
squashed like brittle backs of ladybugs
on the driveway. At naptime your red nails
would snag on small socks.

It would be impossible to read a story
of a girl crossing a bridge in a dark wind
with those red flares lighting the page,
their glare pulling your eyes from the words.
On your typewriter they would flutter
seductive as the secret red underwings of moths
on the brown bark of the keys
distracting you again from words, words black
as loam, that draw you more irresistibly
than any gleaming magnets.

And that is when you would pluck each red poppy,
weed them out, erase them
and go back to the white page
to dig with your bare hands for words
that are the colors of earth and air,
fire and ice and your own flesh.

MARY LYNN H. ELLIS, *NEMCO Branch*

The Lesson

CAROL E. STARK, *Harrisburg Branch*

Waiting is probably the worst part. I have it all in my head and my fingers are ready. Please hurry and be ready for me before something interferes, before a short circuit jumbles the signals and makes it mediocre. Please don't anyone talk to me.

Her mother used to come in and talk to us while we waited. She was so nice. A very small woman with white hair like that angel hair people used to put on Christmas trees, only thicker and in little curled-looking clumps all over her head. She wore one of those flowered aprons ladies her age always wear — tiny blue flowers with red trim all around the edges, the bib of the apron completely protecting the not-so-large, comfortably sunken chest. She usually stood on the over-sized hot air grate in the waiting part of the front rooms. Her skirt would billow up in winter from the slow draft, not Marilyn Monroe style, mind you, but with a gentle consistent fullness as if she might just keep floating on up through the layers of house. But she isn't here any more. People just get old and finally die. It's as simple as that to a ten-year-old. I'm sorry she died. I miss her being here. I think of how empty the house must be for Mrs. Kohler now. Still, I'm glad she's not here right now to distract me.

The last exercise! Finally! It's annoying to follow Suzie Gilmer. She's so technically correct. Those long knobby white fingers just *fly* over the keys. Czerny must be quivering with excitement in his grave. Well, *I* can do it, too. Now, get off the bench and go away and let me have my turn.

Let me have Mrs. Kohler all to myself! I wiggle my way up into position on the over-stuffed green corduroy bench cushion that holds both of us. Some teachers pull up a chair beside you so you can have all the actual piano bench to yourself. Not Mrs. Kohler. She's right there next to you all warm and ample around the thighs. She wears a corset to hold it all in but doesn't feel hard to be next to. I gain confidence from her being right there, touching, generating a kind of deep-in-your-insides current of the success to come in the next ten minutes. I will be brilliant.

We chat. She always likes to chat first. "How's your mother?" "Did she make your jumper?" "Did your choir sing this week?" She tells me a little about some piece she played last Sunday for the organ prelude, but not much. It's as if she's embarrassed to praise herself, although she lavishes it on us.

Once I saw her downtown shopping, bustling from store to store. I thought how strange to see her in the mortal world. Maybe it made me think less of her for a bit. But then it made me warmer to her because she wasn't a figment of my fantasies. Everyone in town knows Florence Kohler.

The disturbing part of that revelation was that she doesn't look like what she is. If someone were to take a picture of Florence and show it to a stranger, he might think she was an aging madam or a senile Southern Belle who never quite made it into the twentieth century. Faulkner would have loved Florence.

She has yellow hair that leans toward pink, like an antique doll in a museum. Her face is very white with a detectable layer of powder and rouge and lipstick to mark where the mouth should extend. She always has on chiffony blouses that reveal the wattled part of her upper arm and lie on her bosom like curtains ready to be poofed by the wind. Her waist is noticeably small, almost out of proportion to her hips. Mother says it's because she never had children and got stretched out. A pair of orthopedic shoes with thickened heels stick out below her neatly tailored and gored skirts — pink skirts, rose skirts, blue skirts that remind you of old silk drapes.

The heels have a purpose. She is an organist — a fine one who doesn't want to be unprepared at any moment to take the four or five strides across the room from piano bench to organ bench. She revels in drawing out a bit of the soul behind the layers of keyboards and stops. Her face always glows when she plays the organ. Her piano brings in her cherished students, but working the organ makes her glow.

It's the way I imagine she glows on those summer bus trips of hers. First, she takes a bus to Princeton for music classes at the end of each July. Then, she takes a tour bus somewhere or other cross-country for a good bit of August. She loves buses, visiting with the people, chatting, smiling, glowing. She gets right out of herself and absorbs the group. She's like a giant sponge that way, drawing in everyone and everything around her. Yet you know you can squeeze and she'll give it all out to the last drop. And then, she'll go right out again and soak up some more of life. But I do get anxious around the beginning of September that Mrs. Kohler has made it back from her voyage safely and is inside the front room on the hill where the trolleys used to run. And the lamp with the green shade is on.

At thirty-eight I still turn my head every time I drive past that house to see if the light is on and the lessons in progress, knowing that Mrs. Kohler has long since been removed to a nursing home and that a new generation of students will not come.

At last! My turn has come to be cherished. To do it right will make her smile all over me and light me up. She'll put a little gold sticker above the title of the piece if I do it good enough, or even pretty close. It'll be square with a little white band across the center with the word "excellent" in red script through the white. I'll be crushed if I don't get one, but I almost always do. If I don't, I'm brave and just tear up a little bit in the car on the way home and pretend my contacts hurt. Mother always buys that since she thinks I'm so "courageous" for wearing them at all at my age. And I whisper to myself that I'll do better next Monday; much, much better. How could I disappoint that woman? She deserves nothing less than all of me for that thirty minutes. I always, *always* get all of her. And I know it. And I always, always will.

Give Yourself Permission

MARY JANE ROTH, *Crafton—Southwest Hills Branch*

Kelly, my daughter who is a recent college graduate investigating the job market, was taking a quiz from a self-help book that was to analyze her personality and suitability for a career.

"Mom," she exclaimed, "listen to my profile: very organized and structured, talented in many things, compassionate with people, supportive and caring. You are also competent and ambitious. Maintaining a lovely, fashionable home is important to you as you treasure what you have worked for. You would be successful at teaching, counseling, social work, or in the medical profession as a general practitioner."

My first impression was how much it sounded like me, and what a marvelous job I had done bringing up my daughter with such positive characteristics.

Kelly then proceeded: "However you are often frustrated because you feel no one really appreciates your talents or realizes how outstanding you are. You feel you are often taken for granted. This anger can prohibit you from being all that you can be. In a leadership position you are inclined to try to do everything yourself. This may jeopardize your success."

This hit home. I remembered being embittered by a handwriting analyst several years ago. He anonymously read my profile at a club program, proclaiming that I made my capital I's much smaller than the rest of my writing. This meant that I did not appreciate myself for my achievements even though I had many. He added, "Perhaps your mother or someone you were trying to please ignored or made little of your accomplishments." What does he know, I thought, but deep inside me a voice said how much the truth hurt. I vowed that I would always let my children know their strengths and always encourage them in their pursuits.

My next conscious reaction to the profile was bewilderment. How could one so young, who had received encouragement, and who had hardly been out in the world yet, reflect so much about women and life? Was she programmed already to live with this anger that so many feel? To add to the complication of it, most are unaware of these feelings. They only know they feel frustration, unhappiness, and unfulfillment. These are usually women that you would consider unlikely to be angry. We all know her, or are her. It is often a person who appears to have everything: an education, a good job, a lovely home, possibly children, a successful husband, and activities outside the home and job. How could these women feel unappreciated or suffer from low self-esteem? When does this start and why is my own daughter revealing a profile of what so many women, so much older than she, display about themselves.

Typical of this is my friend Katie — a nurse, mother of three, former president of three organizations — who never feels she has done enough. "I should be doing more," she will say. "What more can I bring?"

I was finally able to confront this anger and come to terms with it through a job orientation program. As a teacher, I had the opportunity to be part of a teacher center staff. In a nutshell, the job involved meeting with teachers in our school district and being part of a team-sharing experience built around a positive focus of our teaching styles. Everyone has problems, but the main thrust was to share what was done right, not wrong. This was an unusual slant in my profession, as the focus was always the opposite. The principal or supervisor concentrated on what needed improvement. This in itself was well intentioned, but we never heard what we did right. Multiply these events several times a year over a period of several years and on the whole we were facing a great deal of negative, angry teachers.

A realization somehow evolved through this training that my negative feelings were not all my fault and that actually I had survived better than most. My reaction was profound relief. Experience on the job had formerly led me to believe that to negatively question everything on the spot was the way to go. I had berated myself constantly even though it went against the grain of my personality to do so. I am, by nature, an easy-going, flexible person and will usually give anything my best shot before pointing out its shortcomings. The only problem was that anger would build up and I would either hold it in or blow it off at someone whether it applied to them or not. I did overcome the latter, but a lot of anger went against myself and damaged my self-esteem.

From my position at the center, I learned two things. First, my easy-going personality and flexibility were assets. I had to be this way to perform my job well. Secondly, by working with other teachers from a positive standpoint, I found their reactions reflected right back on me. Once we gave ourselves permission to focus on the positive, we learned so much from each other. Many of those examples I use daily in my classroom. Many of those teachers related back to me what I had finally given myself permission to do, feel that I was a great teacher.

The most important thing, though, was that it didn't matter what anyone else thought. I was concentrating so much on them that I never gave myself a second thought. It was so fantastic to see them grow and glow to hear good things about themselves. It didn't happen perfectly every time but it happened enough that I played on my greatest strength: love and enjoy what you do well and so many things will go right for you. Working together made such a difference. I still run into these teachers at meetings and workshops and they remind me of so many pleasant moments shared. Most problems we had were quite minute and easily ironed out when a team of people worked together.

Has everything gone perfectly since? No, but I have so much more confidence to try anything, to really be the best that I can be. I have been applying for advancements and getting to be a real pro at this. I know I won't always get it but I will continue to grow and improve.

I also came to look at my home life from this prospective. I have already achieved almost everything I've ever wanted. My children are almost grown but some work still lies ahead. I know it's going to work out. There have been and always will be problems. It is not what they are, but how you handle them that counts.

So what am I trying to say? Give yourself permission to enjoy life to its fullest. Focus not on what you can't do but on what you can, and do it well. Reflect on your talents and accomplishments, thank God for them, revel in them, and give life your best shot. You will be amazed what this attitude will bring out in other people and how they will reflect back on you. Just don't get envious when they model you and find success themselves.

Soliloquy

You're not going to haul out
that shop-worn bag and
piece by piece take out all
your old flotsam and jetsam
for show and tell!
Didn't you see the tired yawns
last time?

You'd better start little, tiny
because your tinny voice always sings
too serious
amateur theater puffed up too tight
bill-boarding more than it delivers.

No fanfare, no hand-bills
this time just try it word by word
one after another
simple, light
within range.

BERNICE KING, *NEMCO Branch*

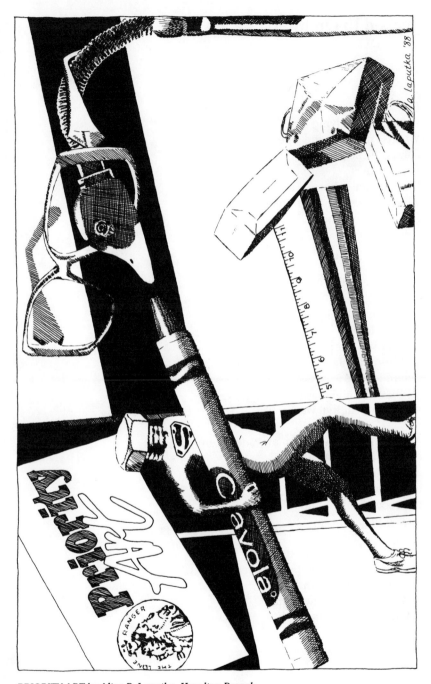

PRIORITY ART by Alice R. Laputka, *Hazelton Branch*

Tucked In On Interstate 79

I'm being driven down a divided highway
through a low lying fog.
Where I'm going and where I've been
cannot be seen.
I welcome
this smaller sphere of sensation
which draws one in upon oneself,
for I feel a heightened
sense of being
tucked in.

As a small child
my frame,
weary from the joy of exploring,
was put to bed
by a caring mother,
and from that act
I emitted
a sense of well-being
for me and all that was

And the stark dawns of many succeeding days
diminished that awe of life
and left raw edges on my feelings
that drove away
the security of feeling
tucked in.

But once that feeling exists
there is always the hope of its rediscovery.
Some have the vision to seek
and some the fortune to find
that peace of being
tucked in.

What course to follow in that pursuit
is both
inward and outward,
that divided highway we all need travel . . .
one's self, others,
work, play, rest,
joy, sorrow
culminates
in that freedom of feeling
tucked in.

And I would imagine in the final analysis
death will be
the ultimate release of feeling
tucked in.

MARTHA MICHAELS VAN HORN, *South Hills Area Branch*

Overheard in Boston

ELEANOR M. MENZEL, *Pocono Area Branch*

Not so long ago in Boston, there was a stately old hotel of pristine white granite called The Bellevue. It was on the "right" side of Beacon Hill (which probably still does have a right side and a wrong side) under the shadow of the State House, seemingly secure from the world.

In its heyday, The Bellevue had enjoyed its share of the well-to-do, but in its last days it was just a decent residential hotel — slightly down at the heel but with head held high, so to speak.

This is the place I preferred to stay when I visited Boston on my own. I loved prowling the old haunts to recapture old memories and feelings. The Bellevue somehow set the mood and I felt comfortable there.

There was a quiet dining room off the lobby for breakfasts and dinners. The carpeting and window drapery may have faded over the years, but were always brushed and clean. Table appointments were replete with damask linen, shining silver, and fresh flowers, although the tables were nearly always empty and served by only two waitresses.

On this particular crisp November morning, I was sipping and savoring their good hot coffee while skimming the *Boston Globe* (to see if my cousin had a byline that day), when I overheard a quiet conversation between a waitress and a woman who also ate alone at a nearby table. (Eavesdropping in restaurants is a favorite pastime of mine — just ask my husband!)

The conversation was really one-sided — the woman did all the talking while the waitress merely commiserated with an "oh" and a "tsk tsk" now and then — so I looked up to catch a glimpse of the speaker.

There sat a frail little woman probably in her late sixties, very expensively if conservatively dressed in a walking suit of hunter green Irish wool. The jacket was folded neatly on the empty chair next to her, along with a wool muffler and matching gloves. She wore a pale green turtleneck sweater with a long string of pearls falling from beneath it.

A cloche hat framed a peaked face with a seemingly sculptured look of bewilderment — brows lifted, deeply set eyes that looked forlorn, a thin straight nose, and a small mouth that smiled furtively. She was not pale, but beautifully made up with just the right amount of blush and eye shadow, and with a trace of lipstick. Actually, she was an attractive woman except for her retiring demeanor. Her hands were thin and fluttery, her nails beautifully manicured and polished. They trembled ever so slightly as she talked, more from a natural reticence than from anything else.

"Yes," she was saying in a breathy, soft-spoken voice, "I did. I lived with my

48

parents my whole life. . . . I mean until they died. I had . . . I had no reason to leave home and live on my own. Even Radcliffe was only a short commute away. Well, to be perfectly honest, I didn't really *want* to leave. The three of us were friends as much as anything else, I had everything I wanted — or at the time *thought* I wanted — and time just passed by unnoticed.

"Oh, I worked after college: I helped translate French manuscripts over in Cambridge for awhile. That was nice. . . ." her voice drifted off a bit.

"Do you speak a language other than English?" she asked, seeming to want to draw in the waitress somehow.

"No, hon, I don't. I wish I had a talent like that, but I do like to listen to music, y'know. Not the heavy stuff, though. Neil Diamond. Barry Manilow. Stuff like that."

"Oh. Yes. I enjoy them, too. I enjoy all kinds of music. After my father died — that was 15 years ago — my mother and I used to attend many concerts of one kind or another. . . . Since Mama died last year, though, I just haven't gone back. . . ."

"I'm sorry to hear about your mother, hon. Want more coffee?"

"No. Thank you. No. Can you understand what I mean — about not leaving home? Does that make sense? It did to me at the time. I mean, we had a lovely large home, I had a suite of rooms and bath all to myself, I tutored many children, I could come and go as I pleased, even when I had suitors." She blushed and looked away. "But then I didn't realize what it would be like once they'd gone. . . . I sold the house and moved here three months ago."

"Well, that's nice, love. I think that's nice."

"Yes, this is a lovely place. But you know, the saddest thing is not losing *them* so much as not finding *me*. All these years. So close to them. I had no need to seek out others — or even seek out ME — and now, at this late date, now, I MUST. So here I am, without financial worries, but without family, without children, without friends, just learning to live."

"Gee, hon, what can I say? You'll do okay; you'll see. Just give yourself a chance. You'll see."

"You're very kind. It's good just to be able to talk to someone who takes the time to listen. Thank you for that. Well, I must be going. The art museum opens at ten o'clock and there is a new exhibit of the Impressionists I've planned to see. Will I see you this evening? No, no, of course not — you're off then. Well, maybe tomorrow morning. I promise I won't talk so much next time."

"Hey, don't feel that way! It's nice talking with you. Really."

"How nice you are. Just be sure you don't end up like me, young lady." She smiled wistfully, got up, slipped on her jacket, her muffler and gloves, adjusted her cloche once, then turned and disappeared into the lobby.

My eyes filled with tears as I, too, slipped away leaving an extra good tip behind.

I didn't see her again. She's gone now. So is the hotel. So are my trips to Boston, except for weddings and funerals. But that last wistful smile and her words remain with me still. Perhaps because, in her own way, she expressed what I — and probably each of us — has felt at one time or another in our lives: that, indeed, each of us is alone, uniquely so. We're just better at making it work for us. And who knows. Maybe she learned to make it work for her, too.

Soliloquy
(from a play not yet written)

HELEN RICHARDSON MEURER, *South Hills Area Branch*

Now I know what you meant, Mama. All those years ago when you said, "I'm not worth the powder and lead. . . ." Your voice trailed off and you didn't finish the "old saying."

I knew it was an "old saying" somehow, but I didn't know what it meant. Ruth, my sister, told me. "She doesn't feel her life is worth the price of the gunpowder and lead in a bullet to blow her head off!" She laughed. I didn't think it was funny, even then.

But now I know what you meant, Mama. Now I know how you felt: used up . . . worthless . . . unneeded . . . abandoned.

All the meals were cooked. All the clothes washed, dried, ironed, and carefully put away. The furniture dusted, the carpets vacuumed. The beds had been made again and again — slept in, made again with sweet-smelling clean sheets to sleep in, to dream on. It seemed like a never-ending job.

But it did end.

Everyone had gone away, giving you a chance to catch your breath, sleep late if you felt like it, and take as long as you wanted to read the paper. To rest, to consider what you might like to eat and to do.

But you found out, as I have: Living and caring for self alone is not enough. It's a kind of freedom but it grows old quickly and is too little to satisfy our need to be a part of this grand scheme of life.

How did you handle all this? I can't remember. I think you went through the same phase I'm just now walking through.

I've been sitting a lot, too, wondering, pondering my past life, my dreams — What were those dreams, Mama? Do you remember? Where did they go?

Sometimes I've stared at the television and at the same time remembered in full detail my conversations with you, with Ruth, with my dearly beloved Bob. He's dead now, too, Mama. He died two years after you. Son Fred has flown the coop to a sunnier clime. He's okay, Mama. I talk to him on the phone, regularly, but he is so far away. Sometimes I've been so lonesome I could die.

Oh, I stay busy with the usual things you have to do to live and get through the day. Friends say I've held up very well. Some know how hard it's been. And everyone says, "It takes time. . . ."

It seems to me I've been waiting for the parts of me that died with each of you, the wounds each left, to heal, to scar over, for the pain to ease a bit.

And it has happened. I wake up glad to be alive. Then I realize I still don't know which direction to move in, with the rest of my life. But there are lots of options.

So, I guess I've spent enough time pondering the universe and wondering about my place in it. It's time to get on with it.

It's time to take a deep breath, pull up my socks, put on my shoes — maybe even buy some new ones! — and get on with it. It's time to find a new place where I enjoy being, where I'm wanted and needed. . . . A new life! It's time to build a new life.

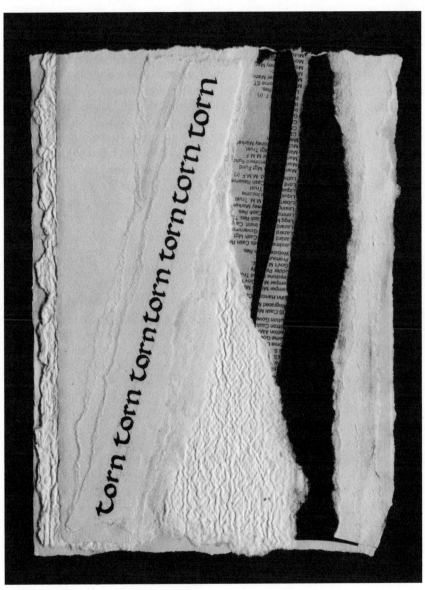

TORN BETWEEN CARING FOR HIM, FOR HER, FOR US — AND FOR ME
by Nancy Douglass, *South Hills Area Branch*

Circus

A circus
Ring of baloney
In the center you preside.
Star of the show
Master of illusion,
Performing tricks of legerdemain
On a tightrope of lies.
Mocking our act
Tossing it away
On the net of infidelity.

A circus
Ring of liberty
In the center I preside.
Star of my show
Master of my life,
Performing solo
Without restraint.
Refining my act
Juggling my freedoms
On a safety net of truths.

ELLA ASTON-REESE, *Crafton — Southwest Hills Area Branch*

At Last . . . Me

CAROL HILLMAN, *Clarion Branch*

I have always been a "people watcher." As a child, I was acutely aware of the roles my parents assumed. My mother was responsible for the child rearing and she delighted in it. She created the most beautiful outfits for me: frilly nightgowns trimmed with lace, green and white polka dotted shorts and halters, flared skirts and blouses with puffy sleeves. If I try, I can still smell Sunday dinner on a clear, cold winter's day: pot roast and potatoes with gravy and applesauce. But what I loved most of all was when she played with me. Memories that elicit feelings of warm security and joy revolve about the times she spent at the ironing board while I sat on the kitchen floor. Together we shaped adventures for my dolls. With sheets and pins, she helped me turn the dining room table into a tent, and seemed to get as much pleasure out of the game as I did.

Mom never tired of telling me stories of her childhood adventures. My favorite was about the time Mom, Aunt Gert, Uncle Gil, and Uncle Len rode across the creek on a haywagon. The horse and wagon ascended the steep bank, but the hay slid off leaving the children stranded and giggling in the middle of the creek! Sometimes when she told me her stories of "the olden days" we would laugh so hard, tears would stream down our faces. I loved to spend time with my mother, but as I grew up I thought of those happy hours as frivolous and of my mother as childlike.

While Mom was fun and always accessible, Dad was serious and more remote. For years he worked two jobs and attended night school, finally finishing college and becoming a CPA. In his few spare hours Dad exercised patience and precision constructing wonders with wood. He made furniture, built a patio and then enclosed it to form a porch. In my eyes the wood my father shaped left as little room for error as he did. After his graduation from college, Dad's greatest desire was to build a house. I shall never forget the summer I spent riding my bike up and down the sidewalk in front of the construction site while Dad built his dream. Everything that went into that structure had to be "the best we can afford." To this day, I get a gripping feeling in my chest when I recall that we had to sell his dream house because we couldn't afford to keep it. Dad had built it too well.

I always wanted to be like my dad. He was so sure of himself, clearly an important person and if he made any mistakes, no one ever seemed to blame him. In my eyes he was perfect and try as I might, I could never hope to satisfy him. I thought that the way to succeed in life was to be serious, goal-oriented, and single-minded in the pursuit of perfection.

55

For far too many years I measured myself against my perception of Dad's definition of success. I don't believe he ever knew how hard I tried to please him. And I don't believe how many years it took for me to sense the futility of that effort.

How can I point to a single event and say, "That is when I realized" . . . or . . . "He gave me the courage" . . . or . . . "They accepted me as I was"? I married a man who is bright and responsible, yet delights in taking time out to be silly. I raised two children who never guessed that I didn't always know what I was doing. Eleven years of teaching gifted youngsters has taught me not only to value the creative process, but to appreciate the child in each of us.

Today I am a women who is sometimes compulsively goal-oriented, incredibly organized, loves to tell funny stories, and cries at graduations and even commercials. I never settle for simply following a recipe, but have to personalize every creation. I have reveled in my children, treasured my marriage, delighted in teaching hundreds of students, and even started my own business. I am creative in everything I do and I am, at best and at last, the sum total of all the lives that have touched my own.

The Bus That Never Came

Two women left their city homes
On that brisk and sunny day.
The bus should stop on the corner
And carry them on their way.

One, lethargic, awaited the bus;
The corner became her fate.
The other, hair flying, heels clicking, said,
"I'll walk — I'd rather not wait!"

She worked her day and then walked back.
The other, drooped, became
One of the shadows waiting
For the bus that never came.

Across the street in sunshine
The smile, the flying hair,
The clicking boots walked homeward
While one sunk in despair.

MARION C. HUTCHINSON, *DuBois Area Branch*

Mary Grey Emmett

PEG DUMBAUGH, *Butler Branch*

This is a big weekend for Mary Grey Emmett.

On Saturday, she'll celebrate her 49th birthday.

On Sunday, the former high school English teacher and mother of three will preach at the 8:30 and 11:00 A.M. services at Mars United Methodist Church, where she is serving as student assistant pastor.

"I couldn't ask for a more gracious, encouraging experience," said Emmett, who is studying for a master of divinity degree at Pittsburgh Theological Seminary. "It takes a real flexibility for a congregation to give this testing experience."

So far, the Butler, Pennsylvania, native hasn't felt any resistance to her plan to become an ordained minister.

"There are those, of course, who aren't sure what to do with me," Emmett said, a warm smile lighting her face. "People aren't sure if it's still okay to talk about recipes."

Emmett spends about 15 hours a week at the Mars church. Her duties include coordinating the youth ministries, participating in the liturgy every Sunday morning, teaching an adult Sunday School class, and preaching about every six weeks.

The Rev. Rodney Smith, pastor of the church, is her supervisor. This Sunday she will preach her third sermon.

Until three years ago, Emmett expected to return to the classroom and teach for the rest of her life. A 1961 graduate of Muskingum College in New Concord, Ohio, where she earned a bachelor of arts degree in English and speech, Emmett taught in the North Hills and former Bellevue school districts and later substituted in the Butler Area School District.

A born communicator, she loved teaching. But there were no full-time jobs available, and she couldn't adjust to subbing for a long period of time.

"It demanded little of me, and it was impossible to set goals. I felt I was in a rut," Emmett said. "The time was right for me to start stretching out. I wasn't at the stage where I could be patient for too many years."

The rut never included being a wife and mother.

"I never had a feeling of cabin fever being home with the children," Emmett said. "It was a creative, wonderful time of my life. I was always involved with the church and community. The walls never closed in."

Raised United Presbyterians, Emmett and her husband John joined First United Methodist Church when they returned to Butler from Middletown, Ohio, in 1980.

"The Methodist Church is wonderfully open," Emmett said. "There's a customary path, but not a rigid path you take."

Two experiences combined to change her sense of direction. First, she began teaching the Bethel Bible Series to an adult class in her church.

"That satisfied a real teaching need for me and made me want to know more about Scripture," Emmett said.

About the same time, she took a graduate course at Slippery Rock University on the teaching of writing. The course caused her to keep a journal and gave her some valuable insights.

Motivated to follow her curiosity, Emmett enrolled at the seminary in September 1984 as a special student and began taking one course at a time.

"I had a real sense that this was what I should be doing," Emmett said. "At the end of the first year, I knew I wanted to do more."

At the seminary, Emmett found a "wonderful, ecumenical atmosphere," not only students from different denominations but also priests and rabbis doing postgraduate work.

Emmett is pursuing her new career with strong support from her husband and children, who range in age from 14 to 22.

"I couldn't do it if they weren't supportive," Emmett said. "They didn't throw up one barrier that would allow me to cop out."

Emmett also gives much credit to her parents, who always encouraged her to grow.

"My first theologian was my dad," said Emmett, the oldest of six children. "I remember sitting around the table after Sunday dinner and being encouraged to think and talk about all kinds of things."

As for her own children, Emmett said, "I wish for them that they matter. If you matter, you are happy."

It is a wish she also holds for herself.

After graduating in May 1989, Emmett will complete a two-year probationary period before being ordained.

Of one thing she is confident: "When this is over, there will be a place for me."

Reflections on Becoming Myself

CAROLE BRIGGS, *Brookville Area Branch*

I'm not one for grouping ministers' wives into some special category and, in fact, tossed aside a recent publication especially for them with barely a "Me-oh-my, another 'poor me' approach to life as a manse-mouse." But then I got to thinking, maybe, after thirty years of success (whatever that means), I have a message that needed telling.

My seminary husband and I did not live anywhere near other seminarians so I didn't participate much in the clergywives meetings (not too many clergyhusbands back then) but I do remember one that I did attend. The wife of a professor spoke and her message was "Be yourself."

That message stuck. Through the coal patches of Pennsylvania, the small town in Ohio, the large city on the Persian Gulf, and the small town in the northwestern part of Pennsylvania, it stuck.

"Be yourself," she said. But thirty years ago, who was I? Daughter, student, wife, and quickly, mother. Soon the student part of my life was squeezed out and my identity seemed to be hinged to the people I was related to. I didn't like that.

Then one Christmas I received a gift. A dear friend offered to babysit once a month. Should I join the choir? Or get more involved in the Women's Association? I choose to join the League of Women Voters and once a month got into political discussion. I didn't ask myself what I ought to do. I asked myself what did I want to do. It was great and I was finding out who I was.

When my children were finally all in school, I found out more about me. I resumed studying (in a new field) and entered the working world. And along the way, I kept that message in the back of my head, "Be yourself."

Being myself didn't mean being insensitive to husband, family, church, and the community around me. It did mean that my needs were important ones to me and that no one was going to really care about my needs unless I let them know what those needs were.

So I remembered that advice and it helped.

It helped when my husband and I were being shown through the church kitchen by the candidates' committee. "And here's the kitchen. I suppose you'll spend a lot of your time here, Mrs. B."

My self really didn't like preparing food for large groups but knew it was necessary sometimes. "No more time than most church members, Mr. Smith."

It helped when a church member knocked on the back door and asked for the keys to the Christian education building. My self didn't like interruptions and knew a paid secretary was in the church office every day. "Oh, Mrs. Jones, you'll have to call the church office and make arrangements for the key. I don't keep one here."

It helped when the Sunday School superintendent asked me to direct the young people's choir. My self knew I had the same twenty-four hours each day as everyone else. "Right now, I'm teaching a primary class, but if you'd like me to give that up, I'll direct the choir. My motto is, one church involvement at a time."

Being myself has meant giving myself space and time to find out who I am. It has meant alienating some, I suppose, and being misunderstood, but I know I cannot be all things to all people, and so have chosen to be me — myself.

At the Child Care Center

MERILYN R. TRUXAL, *Greensburg Branch*

ℳy Mommy and Daddy say they like the way I'm growing. I think I'm growing too. When I learn new things, I feel good about myself. One of the new things I did last year was learn to go to school.

My Mom and Dad both work, so I go to a preschool all day. I'm the first one at school every day, but I like it because my teacher always lets me turn on the girl's bathroom light since I'm the first. She always holds my hand at the door when I wave good-by to my Mom too. Then when she closes the door, she always looks right down at me and says, "Well, Jenny, what shall we do first?" Sometimes, I just want to sit on her lap on the rocker for awhile, and I like to pat her cheeks and say "chubby cheeks" because her cheeks are nice and fat, and she always laughs. Sometimes I like to get a book to read and I don't mind if other kids come in and want to hear it too because she makes sure I still get to sit near her even if the other kids try to move in between. Lots of times she has two kids on her lap and one on each side and some over her shoulder looking at the pictures, but she likes it and I know she does when she looks right at each one of us and her eyes even smile.

Usually when Susan comes in, I like to go and play with her because she's new, but when we're playing and I look over at the teacher, I see her sitting with Devon on the rocker and they're laughing and then I have to go over to see if she still likes to talk to me and she always does, so then Devon and I both sit on her lap on the rocker.

Soon lots of kids are coming in and it starts to get sort of noisy, but I don't mind because Emily and Susan and Rachel and I can get really silly and try on hats and giggle in the mirror and if some of the big boys who are six come by, we giggle at them too, and they mostly don't mind, but I really only like Joey because he lets me look at whatever he brings in to school and never grabs it back like Jonathan.

When everyone is there, the teacher rings a bell and that means to stop and look up at the teacher and be quiet and I always do, but not Jessica. Sometimes she throws a snit, that's what my teacher calls it and she says we have to be patient because Jessica is still growing. That's true because now sometimes she just laughs and stops when the teacher says. Usually the teacher says the bell means to clean up the toys and come to the circle room, but sometimes she says that we're glad to see someone come back who was sick or we should be careful of someone's arm or leg because they got their shot for kindergarten and it might be sore. I always help clean up but not everyone does. Some kids just go right in and get the best chairs, but a teacher goes in and asks them to come back and pick up five toys. I pick up ten toys and then I hurry in so I can sit beside the teacher, but it's too late. I hate that, but then the teacher says I can sit beside Emily, so it's okay unless Rachel and Susan are already beside Emily and then the teacher says we have to "compromise." That usually means I don't get to sit beside anyone I really like. Some kids don't care who they sit beside but Devon always likes to get the blue chair and then her cousin tries to get it too. Somedays it takes awhile to get everyone compromised. When we start singing songs or playing a game, we forget about the chairs, but not Jessica.

After circle time, we have language arts and we each have tables to sit at and some kids never know where their table is until their teacher calls them, but I do so I hurry over to get a good seat beside Emily. We hear stories and learn poems and usually we all like to listen except Jessica who can read already very good, even encyclopedias, so sometimes the teacher lets her read to herself so we can hear the teacher.

Next it's free play and that means we can play in any area we like. I always like the blue area best. That's where the house and play clothes and blocks are, and the climbing ladder but only two can play on that at a time for safety. So we have to take turns. I like Rachel best in the block area because when I have a good idea, she always says "yeah, neat." Some days Emily and I fight because she wants to be the mother all the time. Then a teacher comes over and we might have to compromise again, but not always, because she might suggest we have two families and both be mothers. Or she might say, "We have a problem. What could we do?" I always say I'll be the cat because I really do like to be the cat. Then Emily wants to be the cat too, so we have to change games and start playing zoo or something.

After free play we clean up again and the same kids don't want to, so the teachers have to help them. Then it's group time and I have my own teacher and table again, and we do art projects and papers with alphabet games and numbers and stuff. I like to do papers to take home and I always put them near my bookbag, but sometimes I forget to take them home, or my Mom and I get so busy doing other stuff that I forget to show her my paper. I don't care unless it was really special. I still have lots of papers on my refrigerator. My dad says we need a whole new room just for my papers. I think he's kidding me.

Anyhow, we go out to play at school and the teachers always give the morning kids first turns on the swings so I have to play in the sand or the playhouse because I can still have a turn after lunch. I'm an all-day kid which means I stay for lunch and all afternoon and even cot time.

Lunch is good when I get to sit beside Emily and I like my lunch, only not when it's bologna. Jason's mom and dad always write a note on his napkin, but I can't read yet till I'm in kindergarten next year. I don't need help with my thermos though, only if it sticks, because I'm four. The three-year-olds always need help all the time. I even wipe my mouth with my napkin and I really don't like to eat near Jessica because she's very messy and even sticks her tongue right in her applesauce. She really does and she likes to and some kids laugh, even Rachel, but not me.

When it's cot time, I think about my mom and dad and I miss them. Then the teacher comes and tucks me in and kisses me and I fall asleep while she's reading and while I'm sleeping, my dad comes to school for me. I'm not the last to leave. While I get awake, Daddy talks a little bit to the teacher or the other kids who are awake, and if I want a snack, he lets me finish, but not for too long because we have to go home to start supper before Mommy gets home. In the car, I tell Daddy all the good parts about my school and if anyone was mean to me I tell him too. He always says tell the teacher if you have a problem and I say, "Well, I do, and she'll probably stop the big boys, but if it's a girl, she might say to compromise." Then my daddy laughs and winks at me and I pat his cheek while he's driving and say "chubby cheeks" and we both laugh really hard.

American Women

Women have always worked
    Cooking and canning
    Caring for children
    Tending gardens
    Raising chickens

Women have always worked
    Factory girls losing fingers
    Miners' daughters carrying lanterns
    Female immigrant children doing housework for pay
    Slavery's daughters toiling in the fields

Women have always worked
    Agrarian labor and household labor
    Industrial labor and childbearing labor
    Service labor and volunteer labor
    "Clean" professional labor and illicit sexual labor

Women have always worked
Women have always worked
Women have always worked.

SUSAN DION, *Eastern Delaware County Branch*